GETTING TO KNOW
THE WORLD'S
GREATEST COMPOSERS

G E O R G E
GERSHWIN

WRITTEN AND ILLUSTRATED BY MIKE VENEZIA

CONSULTANTS

DONALD FREUND, PROFESSOR OF COMPOSITION, INDIANA UNIVERSITY SCHOOL OF MUSIC
AMELIA S. KAPLAN, M.A. IN COMPOSITION AND MUSICOLOGY, THE UNIVERSITY OF CHICAGO

CHILDRENS PRESS®
CHICAGO

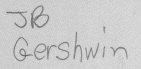
To the memory of my grandmother, Judy Strothers, who helped make music such an important part of my life.

Picture Acknowledgments
Music on the cover, Stock Montage, Inc.; 3, reproduced from the Collections of the Library of Congress, Music Division, George and Ira Gershwin Collection, reprinted with permission of Joanna T. Steichen; 4-5, Private Collection; 7, Culver Pictures, Inc.; 8, Los Angeles County Museum of Art; 16, Culver Pictures, Inc.;17, Billy Rose Theatre Collection, The New York Public Library; 18, courtesy of the Ira and Leonore Gershwin Trusts, used by permission; 19, courtesy of Mrs. Arthur Gershwin; 21, 24, Culver Pictures, Inc.; 26,©Al Hirschfeld, drawing reproduced by special arrangement with Hirschfeld's exclusive representative, The Margo Feiden Galleries Ltd., New York; 27, ©1951 Turner Entertainment Co. All rights reserved; 28, courtesy of Marc Gershwin; 29, Billy Rose Theatre Collection, The New York Public Library; 30, Springer Bettmann; 31 (top), Culver Pictures, Inc.; 31 (bottom), 32, AP/Wide World Photos

Project Editor: Shari Joffe
Design: PCI Design Group, San Antonio, Texas
Photo Research: Jan Izzo

Library of Congress Cataloging–in–Publication Data

Venezia, Mike.
        George Gershwin / written and illustrated by Mike Venezia.
        p.   cm. -- (Getting to know the world's greatest composers)
        For children in kindergarten through 3rd grade.
        ISBN 0-516-04536-9
        1. Gershwin, George, 1898-1937--Juvenile literature.
        2. Composers--United States--Biography--Juvenile literature.
        [1. Gershwin, George, 1898-1937.   2. Composers.]   I. Title.
        II. Series.
        ML3930.G29V46   1994
        780' .92--dc20
        [B]   94-9478
                                                                CIP
                                                                AC

George Gershwin, as photographed by Edward Steichen

George Gershwin was born in New York City in 1898. He became one of America's greatest composers. He is known for his beautiful, exciting concert pieces, as well as for the popular music he wrote for plays and movies.

George was one of the first composers to mix symphonic music with popular music of the day. He came up with a whole new American sound.

At the time George was born, America didn't really have a serious classical music style of its own. Most American composers borrowed ideas from great European composers, like Beethoven, Bach, and Chopin.

George Gershwin, by David Siqueiros. 1936. Oil on canvas, 60 3/8 x 84 1/2 inches. Private Collection

There was a new kind of popular music, though, that was very American. It was called jazz. Jazz was invented by African-American musicians, who used ideas from lots of different styles of music. They often combined work songs from slave times and religious folk songs (called spirituals) with an exciting beat and rhythm. Two other styles of music that helped make up jazz were ragtime and blues. The musicians made up most of the music as they went along, and played the way they felt at the moment. Because of this, notes were never written down, and pieces never sounded exactly the same way twice.

A jazz band in New York, 1919

Cliff Dwellers, a painting of a New York City neighborhood in 1906,
by George Wesley Bellows. Oil on canvas, 39 ¹/₂ x 41 ¹/₂ inches.
Los Angeles County Museum of Art, Los Angeles County Fund

When George was little, New York City was a pretty rough and tough place to grow up in. Neighborhoods were crowded and there weren't many parks or playgrounds around, so kids had to play in the streets. George enjoyed playing street hockey and stickball. He learned to fight pretty well, too, and he was one of the best roller skaters around.

George didn't seem to have much of an interest in music until one day when he was seven or eight years old. George was roller-skating through a neighborhood in New York called Harlem. Harlem was filled with restaurants and clubs where jazz bands played. George never forgot the exciting, lively beat of the music.

He often roller-skated or hitched rides
back to Harlem, just so he could sit outside
of the restaurants and clubs and listen.

A short time later, George heard some classical violin music being played from an open window. He loved the beautiful sound. The kids in George's neighborhood thought only nerds were interested in music.

George didn't care what anyone thought.
After that day, he decided he would learn
everything he could about music right away.

Georgie started going to free concerts,
where he enjoyed listening to classical
music. He even experimented with making
up his own songs on a friend's piano.

When George was twelve, a wonderful

thing happened. His parents bought a
piano. It was really for George's older
brother, Ira. Everyone in the family was
very surprised when George started
playing the piano as soon as he saw it.

Tin Pan Alley, 1914

George was lucky to find excellent piano teachers when he started taking lessons. By the time he was fifteen, he was good enough to get a job playing the piano at a company that wrote songs and printed sheet music. It was in an area of New York City called Tin Pan Alley. Singers and other show-business

Adele and Fred Astaire

people would stop by to listen to new songs
for their acts. It was about the only way
someone could hear a new song, since
there weren't any radios yet, and most
people didn't have record players. George
got to meet some famous people, like Fred
Astaire and his sister, Adele. Sometimes
George played his own songs for them.

My Body,
by Ira Gershwin

George's songs were so lively and fun to listen to that it wasn't long before one of them became a big hit. It was called "Swanee." A famous singer of the day, Al Jolson, heard George play "Swanee" at a party and decided to sing it in his Broadway show. From then on, George found it easier to get jobs writing his own music, instead of just playing the music of other composers.

George sometimes asked his brother, Ira, to write words for his songs. Even though George and Ira were very different types of people, hardly anyone worked better together when it came to making music. George and Ira both enjoyed painting, too. Next to writing music, painting was George's favorite thing to do.

Self portrait of
George Gershwin

George was becoming well known all over New York. He started getting invited to parties given by rich and famous people. Often, George was asked to play his music at the parties. He never seemed to mind, and sometimes played all night long!

One person who liked George's music a lot was a jazz bandleader named Paul Whiteman. Paul thought it was about time to prove that there was important music coming from America and being written by American composers. He decided to put on a serious concert. Paul asked George Gershwin to write a symphonic, jazz-style piece for his concert.

Paul Whiteman and his orchestra

George thought Paul Whiteman's idea
was great. This was his chance to show
how important American music could be.
George called his new musical piece
Rhapsody in Blue. He wanted his music
to have the sounds of modern America,
so everyone could enjoy it.

George wrote parts of *Rhapsody in Blue* while on a train trip. The noise of the steel wheels on the tracks and the train's clickety-clack rhythm gave George lots of ideas for his new music. He often heard music in the noise of machines and traffic and other big-city sounds.

Paul Whiteman's famous concert took place on February 12, 1924. People all over the country tuned in on their radios, and the concert hall was packed.

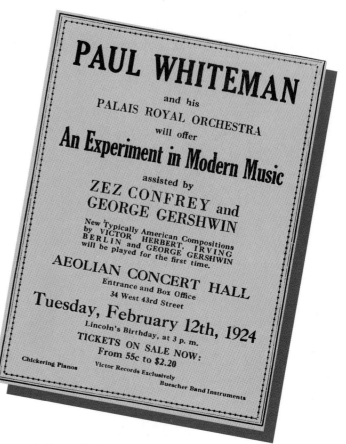

PAUL WHITEMAN
and his
PALAIS ROYAL ORCHESTRA
will offer
An Experiment in Modern Music
assisted by
ZEZ CONFREY and GEORGE GERSHWIN
New Typically American Compositions by VICTOR HERBERT, IRVING BERLIN and GEORGE GERSHWIN will be played for the first time.
AEOLIAN CONCERT HALL
Entrance and Box Office
34 West 43rd Street
Tuesday, February 12th, 1924
Lincoln's Birthday, at 3 p.m.
TICKETS ON SALE NOW:
From 55c to $2.20
Chickering Pianos   Victor Records Exclusively
Buescher Band Instruments

Besides George, Paul had invited several other popular American composers to play their newest music.

For the first hour or so, things didn't seem to go too well. People didn't find the music very new or interesting, and some of them were even getting bored! Then it was George's turn. George was at the piano, and Paul Whiteman led the orchestra.

Hardly anyone could believe their ears.
Rhapsody in Blue began with a clarinet
making a long, whooping, laughing kind of
sound that had never been heard before.
Next, the orchestra joined in, and finally,
George Gershwin began playing.

When it was over, people couldn't stop
clapping. They loved it.

A drawing of Ira and George Gershwin by Al Hirschfeld

Rhapsody in Blue made George Gershwin famous all over the world. He went on to write a lot more music for the theater and movies, much of it with his brother Ira.

Leslie Caron and Gene Kelly in a scene
from the film *An American in Paris*

Many of George and Ira's songs became
hits, and are still popular today. George
continued to write symphonic music, too, like
Concerto in F and *An American in Paris.*

George Gershwin's favorite musical piece was his opera *Porgy and Bess*. An opera is like a play, except the actors sing instead of speak the words. *Porgy and Bess* was different from other operas, though. It was about poor African-American fishermen who lived in a waterfront area of South Carolina called Catfish Row.

Program from a production
of *Porgy and Bess*

George Gershwin's sketch of his room
at Folly Beach, South Carolina

George traveled to South Carolina and
stayed near the people he was writing
about, so he could learn more about them
and make his music sound really authentic.

When *Porgy and Bess* first played in New York City, some people didn't like it. They weren't sure if it was a serious opera, or a play, or a musical comedy.

George was disappointed. He knew his opera was probably the best thing he had ever done.

A tense moment in
Porgy and Bess

George explained in a newspaper article that *Porgy and Bess* was a new kind of opera—a folk opera. It was about real, everyday people. The opera's *music*, too, was like the lives of real people. Sometimes the songs were fun and happy; other times they were serious or sad.

Over the years, people began to understand *Porgy and Bess*. Today it is one of the world's most popular operas.

A scene from a 1943
production of *Porgy and Bess*

31

George Gershwin (left) and his brother Ira (far right)

George Gershwin died in 1937. His music sounds as new and exciting today as it did when he first wrote it. Sometimes George used other things besides instruments to get just the right mood or sound. In *An American in Paris,* he used real taxi horns. In *Second Rhapsody*, he even used a fly swatter!

The best way to get to know Gershwin is to listen to his music. Since it's as popular as ever, it's pretty easy to find it on the radio. You can also borrow tapes and CDs at many libraries.

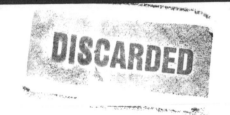